Enchantment

DAVID MORLEY is an ecologist and n
has won fourteen writing awards and p
Prize, the Poetry Business Competi
Writer's Award, an Eric Gregory Awai
a Hawthornden Fellowship. His pre
(Carcanet, 2007) was a Poetry Book Society Recommendation. ... .
known for his pioneering ecological poetry installations within natural landscapes and for the creation of 'slow poetry' sculptures and I-Cast poetry films. His 'writing challenges' podcasts are among the most popular literature downloads on iTunes worldwide: two episodes are now preloaded on to all demo Macs used in Apple Stores around the world. He has performed his poems and stories at many of the major literary festivals. He writes essays, criticism and reviews for the *Guardian* and *Poetry Review*. A leading international advocate of creative writing, he wrote *The Cambridge Introduction to Creative Writing* and is co-editor with the Australian poet Philip Neilsen of *The Cambridge Companion to Creative Writing*. He currently teaches at the University of Warwick.

Also by David Morley

POETRY
Releasing Stone
A Belfast Kiss
Mandelstam Variations
Clearing a Name
A Static Ballroom
Scientific Papers
Ludus Coventriae
The Invisible Kings
The Rose of the Moon
The Night of the Day

NON-FICTION
Under the Rainbow: Writers and Artists in Schools
The Cambridge Introduction to Creative Writing

EDITOR/CO-EDITOR
Northern Stories 2
The New Poetry
Of Science
The Gift
Phoenix New Writing
No Longer Poetry: New Romanian Poets
Collected Poems of Geoffrey Holloway
The Greatest Gift
The Cambridge Companion to Creative Writing

E-MEDIA
Writing Challenges
Slow Poetry
'Poetry Challenges'

DAVID MORLEY

Enchantment

CARCANET

First published in Great Britain in 2010 by

Carcanet Press Limited
Alliance House
Cross Street
Manchester M2 7AQ

Copyright © David Morley 2010
Illustrations on pp. 25 and 47 copyright © Peter Blegvad 2010

The extract from Duncan Williamson, *Fireside Tales of the Traveller Children* (Canongate 1985) on p. 27 is included by permission the Estate of Duncan Williamson

The right of David Morley to be identified as the author of this work has been asserted by him in accordance with the Copyright, Designs and Patents Act of 1988
All rights reserved

A CIP catalogue record for this book is available from the British Library

ISBN 978 1 84777 062 2

The publisher acknowledges financial assistance from Arts Council England

Typeset by XL Publishing Services. Tiverton
Printed and bound in England by SRP Ltd, Exeter

To my mother, Rose

with rocks, and stones, and trees.
William Wordsworth

Acknowledgements

Acknowledgements are due to the editors of the following publications in which these poems first appeared: 'The Lucy Poem' in *Feeling the Pressure: Poetry and Science of Climate Change* (edited by Paul Munden, British Council, 2007); 'Alaskan Salmon', 'Mayflies' in *Horizon Review*; 'Abandoned Christmas Tree Plantation', 'Colin Clown', 'Demelza Do-It-All', 'Dragonflies', 'Port Meadow, Oxford, 1983', 'The Water Measurer', 'Zhivakos the Horseman' and the opening forty lines of 'The Library Beneath the Harp' in *The London Review of Books*; a complete version of 'The Library Beneath the Harp' in *Long Poem Magazine*; 'Hedgehurst' in *PN Review*; 'Nightingales' in *The Poetry Paper* (The Poetry Trust); 'Camargues', 'The Circling Game', 'Skeleton Bride' and 'Spinning' in *Poetry Review*; 'Moss Eccles Tarn, Far Sawrey, 1983' in *The North*; 'Papusza' in *Polarity*; 'Proserpina' in *The Rialto*; 'Chorus' and 'Taken Away' in *The Wolf*. Six poems were published as a pamphlet, *The Rose of the Moon*, which was one of the prizewinners of the 2009 Templar Poetry Pamphlet Competition. Some poems were issued as part of a limited edition by Nine Arches Press as *The Night of the Day* (2009). Some poems (and fragments within poems) were part of a 'Slow Art Trail' commissioned by Chrysalis Arts sited within Strid Wood in Bolton Abbey, some of which were released as poetry films on iTunes and www.youtube.com by the University of Warwick.

    Many thanks to a magician of ink, word and sound, Peter Blegvad, for responding to the poems and creating two images and a cover; to Chrysalis Arts for a commission; and to Phil Brown, Peter Carpenter, Jane Commane, Peter Davidson, A.L. Kennedy, China Miéville, Philip Neilsen, Fiona Sampson, Daniel Soar and George Ttoouli for editorial help; to Dan Allum and the Romany Theatre Company; and to members of Peter Jolly's Travelling Circus. I am grateful to the University of Warwick for a period of research leave during which this book was completed. My deepest thanks, as ever, go to my wife Siobhan Keenan for her support and love.

    Enchantment is the final book of a three-part cycle of poems, the first two parts of which were *Scientific Papers* (Carcanet Press, 2002) and *The Invisible Kings* (Carcanet Press, 2007).

Any Romany or Parlari (circus language) is given in English translation at the foot of the page. The alphabet used in Romany language is phonetic.

Contents

Fresh Water	11
The Lucy Poem	17
Chorus	20
Proserpina	21
Abandoned Christmas Tree Plantation	23
Hedgehurst	27
Taken Away	37
Romany Sarah	39
The Circling Game	40
Camargues	46
The Library Beneath the Harp	49
Nightingales	57
A Lit Circle	58
Spinning	69
Skeleton Bride	73
Notes	81

Fresh Water

in memory of Nicholas Ferrar Hughes, 1962-2009

Port Meadow, Oxford, 1983

Walking to Woodstock Road from Wytham Wood
where leaf-worlds welled from all the wood's wands,
we talked salmon, midges, floodmeadows, the energy system
cindering softly under us, slow-cooking the marshlands.
The gate ought to be here. The map said so.
That map back at my flat… Look, there's a spot
somewhere this way where sheep shove through.
See those fieldfares and redwings? They landed last night.
Then a step within a fence nobody bothered with for years
or knew, except the sheep. So Nick stepped up
and through, and there on the other side, two horses
with thrilled-up ears, barged him skilfully to a stop.
I said that gate was around here – pointing a mile or two.
Worth the way – Nick's arms across both horses – *to know these two.*

Dragonflies

This water's steep and deep. There are signs in artery red.
Their letters pump with advice. But it's June and we have trod
ourselves senseless sampling some imaginary species of coleoptera…

So, there are our cautions slung down like life-vests by the river
and with stone-drop certainty we launch out from a hanging ledge
to collide with a chill so stinging it was like flinging your body
into a bank of nettles. Then head-butting the surface to see
at eyelash-level the whiphands of Common Backswimmers surge
and sprint, each footing a tiny dazzle to prism.
                                                            Then these
sparking ornaments hovering then islanding on our shoulders
each arching its thorax into a question: what is the blue
that midnights all blue? How can crimson redden before you?
The old map mutters that Here Be Dragons, and it lies.

Here be Darters, Skimmers, drawn flame. Here, are Dragonflies.

The Water Measurer

We could have watched him until our watches rusted on our wrists
or the tarn froze for the year's midnight. The Water Measurer
struck his pose and recalibrated his estimates as if he had misplaced
his notebook, or perhaps his mind, with all that staring at water.

Why does he walk on it with such doubt and mismeasure
when he has the leisure of hydrophobia (those water-fearing hairs
on the undersides of his legs)? Maybe that is his secret,
that he doesn't know his step will never or not quite penetrate
the depth below, glowing with prey and the upturned eyes
of predators. Does he ever get any of this right? Is he unwise?

He tests and counts, counts and tests, in pinprick manoeuvres,
never satisfied with the data of darkness or statistics of sunlight.
It seems he holds his nose at the thought of getting it right, or of not
getting it not right, never or not quite like the water-fly in *Hamlet*.

Mayflies

Where are we going tonight with our fine-meshed nets
and sampling grabs? Into the rain of all rivers, and the sea
of all weathers. Our jeep does the graft of our feet.
We rev and jerk down the tracks on the back of a planet.
River and banks are an interchangeable blackout. We proceed
by feel so as not to light alarm. We drag the riverbed out,
capsize its stone babies on our sampling tray, then ignite
their whole world in unravelling, incinerating light.

It is night's nursery below stunned stones on the stream's bed
where even the darkness is felt in minuscule spirals
that swirl from the larval mayfly's feelers: a code,
unmade from sand grain and rain and particles
that swerve through this under-space like quiet comets,
each considered and caught or flung on a fresh trajectory.

Alaskan Salmon

An angler casting in line with the fish's cast. His wrist halts,
top-locking the reel – a fist freezing over another live fist -
until the water's worn door slaps open on its hasps…
Salmo salar – those lights that leapt from the solar flare
of a mid-Atlantic lighthouse; that swum – or strummed
to landfall with rumours of petrels – of shearwaters
pashed against the spun sun of that high prism.

To landfall – to riverfall, then waterfall – a slown, sure
skimming stone on ladders of sheered water:
those envoys of an oceanic storm, *Salmo salar*,
coiling against arcing voltages of an Alaskan river,
springing at their height like bending wands
casting themselves towards its spawning grounds,
plashing gradients until they nose the river's birthing vaults.

Moss Eccles Tarn, Far Sawrey, 1983

I'd backed the van downhill when it should have been uphill
which meant an evening's field trip to observe emerging midges
became a nightlong skin-close study of their feeding habits.

Nick will back me up in this – when we finally get the van to roll
against its natural earthward loll, when the farmer comes by
at five with fodder and the god-like strength of his tractor –

that we'd come up with every practical solution for the insoluble:
flotsam, rocks and clothing between wheels and churning mire;
balances of broken branches acting as a jack, or dry dock;

and then wisdom dawned across the fields just before four
so we dozed an hour, under the radar of owl and nightjar,
under the nose of the mole, shrew and burrowing badger,

in earshot of the fox clattering through bracken at a woodcock
and woke above clouds that had collapsed to the valley's floor.

The Lucy Poem

'Lucy', *Australopithecus afarensis*, 3.2 million years BC

As her eyes accommodate
  from the billion-leafed glitter
of deep jungle, the walker
  spies prayed-for water where
the sun bounces like a saiga
  off the savannah.
This is fresh to her:
  to watch forwards rather
than clamber to seek. Sand grains
  slither under her slim feet.
Despite the drowsing civets
  and wild dogs, she steps her
soft track behind her clear
  so her friends might follow.

She can sense as much water
  in her breasts as in the earth;
except there is a denial of water
  even in ground-air: only whorls
of liquefied heat you find above
  elephant-tracks or the tread
of limestone beds. Tiny streams
  start at the hoof point of beasts –
mirages and fractured mirrors.
  On the plain she glimpses
air-rivers and flat inland oceans
  of light above which mountains
flicker: arks of snow wrecked
  on their crowns – the roof
of Africa, sunstruck then shadow-
  halved then forestial
with star-flowers. To her
  those highlands seem
an escape of stone, an island
  blown inland by the simoom,

 dust-devils spinning the land
  grain by grain into place.

Her mother's stories tell how
 when those mountains
bloomed from underworld lodes
 springing geladas led their fat
appetites to the snow-caps
 muscled like woolly gods;
and then the gorillas lurched
 through the forests to steal
their high hammocks. Her mother
 believes the star-flowers
shrove the geladas, scolded them;
 those monkey-gods were elved now,
scarced in shape. The summits
 themselves diminished too:
they wept so hard they
 no longer kept the season
but wore their water as snow-
 necklaces, ice-pearls…

When the waterhole went
 wolves ran with their thirsts
higher than fur could manage:
 they loped the dry courses
to their source, lapping parched
 stone where water buried its song
and as they pounded upwards
 seeking the wet tongue
of that voice, so the geladas
 skittered, bounding higher
up that mountain roof
 until they regained the snow
and turned to stare
 from its gleaming ridge.

The wolves fathered
  a line of grey wolf-stones
below the snow, staked
  them for years, while below
the plains wilted to sand;
  the forest breathed
its leaf-litter in and out
  until one day it breathed in
maggots and breathed out
  blowflies, and our walker woke.

Overhearing melt-water
  our walker wakes; she balances
her thirst against the night's dew,
  steadies herself to the climbing
track, unloads her steps behind her
  one by one. Shadows moisten
her heeled hollows; the moon's
  sun sets her prints as stone,
and she senses herself neither
  walk nor walker, striding the hill
in the light of all she knows –
  geladas guarding the white
heights; star-flowers
  glistening in crevices;
the crouched wall
  of wolves;
the high snows,
  their wells
of prayed-for
water.

Chorus

on the birth of Edward Daniel Keenan Morley

The song-thrush slams down gauntlets on its snail-anvil.
The nightjar murmurs in nightmare. The dawn is the chorus.
The bittern blasts the mists wide with a booming foghorn.
The nuthatch nails another hatch shut. The dawn is the chorus.
The merlin bowls a boomerang over bracken then catches it.
The capercaillie uncorks its bottled throat. The dawn is the chorus.
The treecreeper tips the trees upside down to trick out insects.
The sparrow sorts spare parts on a pavement. The dawn is the chorus.
The hoopoe hoops rainbows over the heath and hedgerows.
The wren runs rings through its throat. The dawn is the chorus.
The turnstones do precisely what is asked of them by name.
The wryneck and stonechats also. The dawn is the chorus.
The buzzards mew and mount up on the thermal's thermometer.
The smew slide on shy woodland water. The dawn is the chorus.
The heron hangs its head before hurling down its guillotine.
The tern twists on tines of two sprung wings. The dawn is the chorus.
The eider shreds its pillows, releases snow flurry after snow flurry.
The avocet unclasps its compass-points. The dawn is the chorus.
The swallow unmakes the spring and names the summer.
The swift sleeps only when it's dead. The dawn is the chorus.
The bullfinches feather-fight the birdbath into a bloodbath.
The wagtail wags a wand then vanishes. The dawn is the chorus.
The corncrake zips its comb on its expert fingertip.
The robin blinks at you for breakfast. The dawn is the chorus.
The rook roots into roadkill for the heart and the hardware.
The tawny owl wakes us to our widowhood. The dawn is the chorus.
The dawn is completely composed. The pens of its beaks are dry.
Day will never sound the same, nor night know which song wakes her.

Proserpina

'I could write a cliché about conservation here
but I won't and I won't because I can't.' The gesture
politics of that dead elm is sufficient and your own
reasons for driving above walking and mine for typing
on a laptop under fake light and not a typewriter
under an electric summer noon.
                                   Where does it get us,
this wood, and these winding paths so like the paths
we'd like to make through the woods of our lifetimes
with their borders on the unsure growth but clear
and cleared to make our movements easier, our voices
lower, below the half-lit and otherworldly leaves?

There's a viewpoint in this conversation like the viewpoint
we are standing at overlooking that landfill, the sight at first
as insolent as a chainsaw in the chest of the fells
until you hear about how the fell-side is dug then double-dug
by the great gardeners in their bulldozers.
                                          It is true
that what we waste bends back to grind us. My rubbish
is also here in me, and I shove and shovel it around
every day, sometimes alert to its weight and stench
but most of the time too busy or bored to see or scent
the wealth and ruin of evidence, its blowflies, the extended
families of vermin. Much of that time you won't notice it either
unless you take against me which I'm hoping this conversation
might prevent. As you say, if somebody takes against you
there's no landfill can hide you or me, dig us, double-dig us
into cleansing soil.
                     So we wonder why we took against
                            that fell-side, and against
these woods and small rivers; why did we move against
the limestone to scrape it into cinemas and chapels;
kick against the ferns in favour of a few sheep; against
the dale, chain-ganging its stones like they were criminals?
The Ice Age had a knack for natural sculpture: that terminal
moraine and limestone pavement, that scarp and shelf,

those Scars and tarns – these were artistic successes, won
no awards; we bulldozed them like tower-blocks.
                                             We are not
mistakes on this planet which is why I could write a cliché
about conservation here but I won't. Maybe you and I
who have never met are caught in no choice, separate strands
of sheep wool snared on a wire fence, blown and soaked,
sunned until we rot, unable to see or hear each other
but sensing the iron thorn angled through our spines.
                                                        Move,
I want to say, talk to me across these winds.
We are dying out here together. There is more we could do
if we would curve to each other, to attend as Ruskin did
to Malham Cove when the stones of the brook were softer
with moss than any silken pillow; the crowded oxalis leaves
yielded to the pressure of the hand, and were not felt;
the cloven leaves of the Herb Robert and robed clusters
of its companion overflowed every rent in the rude crags
with living balm; there was scarcely a place left
by the tenderness of happy things where one might not
lay down one's forehead on their warm softness and sleep.

Ellar Carr Hill, walking between Strid Wood and Embsay

Abandoned Christmas Tree Plantation

We are waiting for a Christmas that never came,
each species a friend of a friend of some needle-hue.
All the years, heights and postures are present
like children in a school that no child ever leaves.

Each species a friend of a friend of some needle-hue:
those adolescent spruces prickle with boredom
like children in a school that no child ever leaves.
The infant firs sing to themselves in the snow.

The prefect pines, sky-high, peer down unmoved.
Those adolescent spruces prickle with boredom;
the infant firs sing to themselves in the snow.
We speak through the wind and only then in murmurs;
stretch our limbs into the wind to catch at birds.

The prefect pines, sky-high, peer down unmoved
bartering a bullfinch song for a goldfinch chime.
We speak through the wind and only then in murmurs.
By dusk we are whispers and secret playtime rhymes.

We stretch our limbs into the wind and catch at birds.
Our tree rings are school bells that peal in December
bartering a bullfinch song for a goldfinch chime.
By dusk we are whispers and secret playtime rhymes.

All the years, heights and postures are present.
Our tree rings are school bells that peal for December.
We are waiting for a Christmas that will never come.

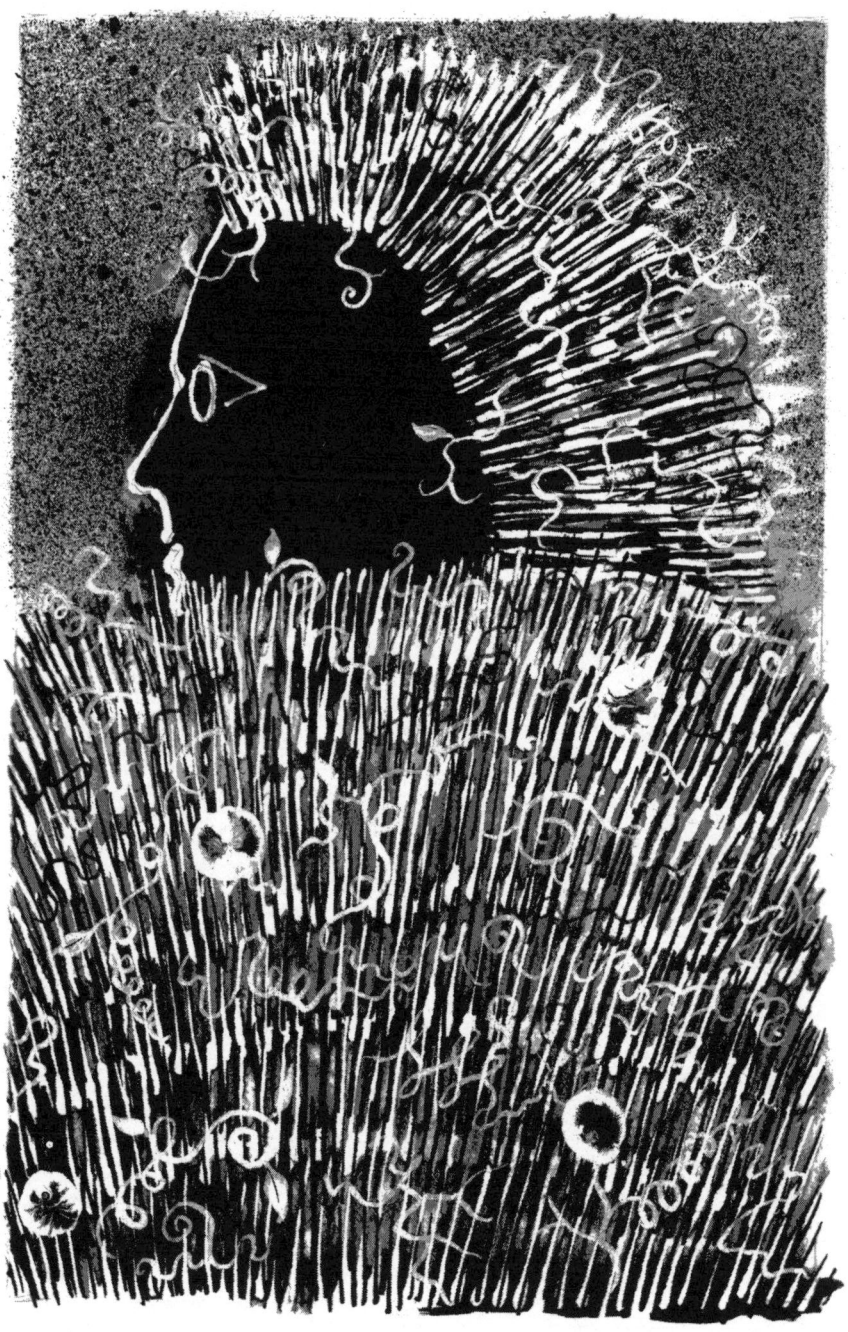

Hedgehurst

Romany

So out stepped this young man – half hedgehog and half human being. And the king stood and looked: he'd never seen a creature like this in all his days.

He said, 'What type of being are you that could do all this? Have you anyone to help you?'

'No', said the hedgehurst, 'I need help from no-one.'

'You mean to tell me', says the king, 'that you built this place by yourself and you cut all these trees, built all these things and made this place like this?' It was the most beautiful place the king had ever seen.

'I have', said the hedgehurst, 'I've done all this myself. But anyway, getting back to you: what is it you want of me, for I am king of this and this is my kingdom.'

'I want nothing from you', says the king. 'But I am amazed! Tell me, what are you?'

He said, 'I am a hedgehurst.'

Duncan Williamson, *Fireside Tales of the Traveller Children*

I am Hedgehurst. I, snow-
slumbering, the loaf of my body
ovened in a bole beneath
a flame-leafed sycamore,
uncurl from my coiled hole.
Whose is this scorned skin?
What weather rouses me
to lag my limbs with lichen,
to fold fresh thatch around me?
I roll, I loll in fallen leaves.
They melt me asleep; I
blunder through dream,
weaving that way then this,
from Februaries of thawing
to nodding November.
My mind measures out claw points,
paw prints but snarls me into a ball.
A jury of jays jabs me, scolds me.
Why are you dozing here? they jabber.
What, what is, what is your story?

Born blunt, born blind, I pawed
the mist of my mother,
sensed her shawl around
me like leaf-dry shelter.
Her love, a raw rend across
her womb; she wore my birth
along her thighs in rips, in wounds.
Childless, she had chided
my father in tears, in years,
until overheard by a wider world –
in the sleight of a stranger who
held a hedgehog on her palm,
who smiled her spell through
their walls. Worlds were unspun.
I nosed through that cottage
for six years, eye-high to its locks.
Outside, my father's axe lit
lightning from the oak's flint barks.
When I found my feet
I floundered forwards on all fours.

My father flared and fumed as
I fumbled with gravities.
I lapped spilled milk while he
watched me, as wary as a hare.
My bed was strewn stale straw.
I lay still on my spines'
springs, napping on my nails.
My father's weasel whine
seeped and stole through
my rough wall each drab night.
My mother's muteness was enough
to shut me into some bright
burial ground of myself, to grind
her halved child into ground.
I was space between an axe-edge
and the oak's white wound.
I was seven in nothing but age
when I left home with no word.
I wound my way through the walls
of their world and into this wood.

The tines of my pelt, draggling,
made me stronger as I went;
and, when I made camp,
found myself no stranger
to that wood's world. I called
my name into the night. The trees
shushed me, then answered
with caterpillars baited on threads.
I called again. Moths moored
in bark-fissures flickered out,
fluttered towards me as I spoke
as though my voice were alight.
Pipistrelles unfurled through firs.
Fireflies bloomed and doused.
I called until dawn into the next
dawn. I spun and unspun their names
with my name. When I had worlded
the woods with these creatures
I lounged on my spines.
I then called out the birds.

Clamorous as alphabets in a cloud,
starlings strew down. They settled
like a harvest in the highest
trees and sang, drizzling.
Then came magicians, green
woodpeckers, the greenest men.
They were circling laughter. They
were soft rolls on the oak's drum.
Ceremonially stabbing his prey
on haw, sloe, dog rose,
a shrike shrieked down to feast,
his larder stiff on thorns.
Woodpigeons unwarped their wings,
clapping through larch canopies.
Wrens buzzed from bushes. Tree-
creepers moused down yew-
towers. Rolled bodily from a nest
a solitary cuckoo came
closer than comfort, bearing
her unchilding charm.

Arcing down the air's stair silently,
those emblems — snowy owls
bowed whitely then blinked.
In the brimming underworld below
their bowing branches, ptarmigans
moved, still smooth with snow.
I kept my call up — the starlings
now imitating — so I swerved it,
narrowed it, arrowed my voice
down the bolt-holes of hedgerows,
calling up the fields and the further
afields of floodplain, lake, river.
A tarn's surface flickered with the ore
of rudd, orfe and roach.
Dace, carp, and loach spun
on their rudders to the fly of my call.
I viewed the arc of my kingdom:
a rainbow righting itself above water,
its likeness mirrored and ringed
under and above the surface of all things.

I latticed hedges in high tension
about the wood's borders,
their branches barred, all twigs
cats-cradled. No low doors for badgers.
No runnels for runaways. Even roots
rammed deeper. Those windows
between leaf and leaf I made
shatter-proof with web and web, spiders
garrisoning them like a million eyes
in a wall. For twenty years I had peace
when a door unlatched where no door
was, its hasps hidden in a space
of a second guess. Striding in circles
of his own dream, a hunting king
came upon my clearing while I crafted;
needling me for directions, marvelling
at my work. I needed help from no one,
so returned that king to his kind,
he, gifting his word that the first thing he saw
within the world elsewhere would be mine.

I had kenned from my wrens
how to cave-mine my call,
to speak through soil, make
speech slither through a hill,
and I learned from my bats
and owls how to hear it all back,
the echo resounding slow
in the swirl and swoon of a beck,
given tongue as it trickles from
rock-pool to spill murmurs
along a lake-bed, passed through
caddis fly to bloodworm to fish
before the catch is ospreyed
up from the water and sprayed
back through the nets in my ear.
In this way I overheard
the worlds outside my wood:
how the king had come home,
how his daughter, his dearest child,
had been the first to greet him.

But no word reached me. I let
the seasons sing themselves slow.
I let the winds wind through
on their migrations. I lay
my ear to the lake and listened.
Silence and then ice. Jays
mocked me to life in March.
I rose and called twice
for what it would take –
I called all my creatures.
I could make war with water,
by damming ducts, flash-floods,
by underwhelming wells but I
could not take a field with fish.
I had noise enough to light out
for territory – snipe's throb, woodpecker's
drum, stork's clack, heron's bill-clap,
and at dawn, the lapwing's thrum.
The birds went before me, and my army,
the earth's creatures, they followed me.

Fat rain soaks an unwringable soil.
The sun's hand fumbles at a rag
of earth. It can do nothing with it
but shape steam or ice. The slog
of roots as they ply through rock,
murk, moisture – this was my work
that half-day. When rain runs
over rain, when deep roots are delved,
high banks breached, the araucaria's
canopy's reefed, leaf-land on a lake,
drench-drowned, its green throat
gasping; so it was when we
showed up at that king's fences
and forts; he, done over in a
heartbeat, his whole kingdom
drowned by hoof-beats, antlers
clattering in his pallid palace;
and his people, his, peering
from their portholes, from
prison ships of their tenements.

Leaves allow answers to a season:
when to give way, when to hold
hard. I had these humans
in the hands of my branches.
I held them up to the spring:
showed them the month's doors
opening on each other, those
rain-crafted courtyards of a year;
offered them the openings
of a fern, the currencies
of those smote-eyed seeds;
gave them the conditions
written in grass-blades
as a wind wicks through them;
read softly the rules
of the rain as it retreated
to its ravines and rivers;
and when this was done
the king's daughter came to me
without question or ambition.

In the broken and in the woken
dreams of the king's people
I moved to teach the tongues
torn from them: my creatures' calls.
In the palace hall, the court spoke
at me on their stilts of speech;
I scythed those sticks: tottering
tongues stammered and spilled.
In the city I was the space
between a shrike's spike and prey.
I was a holly bush among them.
Carnivalled in star-lit nails
I nightwalked the city. Will
to will, my wife met me,
while the silk king sulked.
For its wands of low light
to wane through the windows
to douse my blood, to slow me,
to slow me so and so clench me
that coward king waited on winter.

My beasts were busy unweaving
and reweaving the city: wood wasps
worked the wrecked timbers
of the tenements, ravens
refreshed the roofs. Snipe,
scaup and scoter settled
at reservoirs, sweetened inrunning
rivers, drilled then dredged
the silts and sands. Crossbills
and finches fossicked field-seed;
horses hauled those harvests home.
I foddered my creatures by starlight
steeling my skin against the moon's
zero. My hearth held some secrecy
of spring: to win through winter
I would need that fire's hand.
Each night I knelt nearer its blaze.
I strained with my spines. I stripped
myself clear of my cladding, then
made my way numb beneath the moon.

Three nights with my nerves
on knives; three nights clad
in the cold's clay; my hearth,
pelt and wife waiting for me at dawn.
I was almost blunt and blind,
my mother's mist rising
as I yanked fodder to the stalls
calling creature to creature.
On the third midnight I plucked
then placed my pelt. My wife
watched from our bed then
waving once, wondered to sleep.
I staggered through a sheer snow
of stars. I made everyone safe.
I smelled before I saw my broad
skin broiling where the king
had stoked it high on a bonfire.
And then the king came to me,
soldiers before him, bright buckets
jagged and acid with ice-water.

The water's wile, the wound of it,
it winded my mind; its ice spermed
through my veins, hatched in my heart.
Breath blew from me and I fell
into a glacier of my blood. I saw
the king handed my father's axe;
my wife running from her room,
out from dream; and then
his daughter flying at him, bearing
down on a boar, her white
wrists writhing. All this. I saw all this
before a wind flew back through me
and I whispered my wife's name.
The stars shushed me, then
answered me with caterpillars
baited on threads. I called her again.
Moths stirred in bark-fissures.
They flickered out, fluttered
towards us as I spoke her name,
as though my voice were a light.

Overheard by a wider world
I called the kennings of the people: spun
and unspun their names, emparadising them,
shaping, smiling a spell through their walls –
Adder and Anemone　　　Badger and Bear
Corncrake and Curlew　　　Deer and Dragonfly
Earwig and Elver　　　Fox and Firecrest
Grebe Grasshopper　　　Hoverfly Hare
Ibis and Iguana　　　Jackdaw and Jay
Kittiwake Kingfisher　　　Lapwing Lacewing
Mole and Merganser　　　Nuthatch and Nightjar
Oriole and Otter　　　Pike and Plover
Quail Rabbit Ruff　　　Smew Salamander
Twite and Turnstone　　　Urchin and Viper
Wryneck Wheatear　　　Yaffle and Zander
worlding the king's people with the coats
and calls of these creatures, weaving
halls and walls into our woods
and when this was done
their world was mine.

Ramsons whiten into life, slow-
slumbering through the thaw.
After spring showers, my halved
children will tread paths sprung
and sewn from their scent alone.
I wake half-dreaming. For seconds
I do not know myself. What hands
are these that are lacerable
but sprung with spines?
What weather rouses me,
unclenches my limbs from frost?
Where is my second skin?
It is winter gone.   It is worlds unspun.
I judder awake as jays bounce
and strut about my body.
I rise, I shout, and they scatter.
They jump screaming into the sky.
It is time to call everything to life
for I am king of this and this is my kingdom.

Who am I?   I am Hedgehurst.

Taken Away

The mother places her baby at the waterfall's brim.
She waits for the moon's climb.

They'd been hard at the hay with a blunt scythe between them
circling and slashing for hours under blanking sunlight
with the cradle nestled and nooked on the one hayless place.
They'd had their breakfast, porridge and milk and tea,
scones, cheese, whatever they had. Their picnic things
were scattered on the green knowe around the cradle
as if plates and pots and pans had been tossed out by the baby.

The wife shadows her husband with a wide wooden rake
weaving and whirling his handwork as he worries the hay loose.
You know how a man makes bouts of hay with a scythe
and round and round the field in close and closing spirals
he rounds on the hayless knowe and that one white cradle
with cups and greaseproof wrappings pallid with butter;
like a maze of mauve leading into a green eye and an unseen
staring gap among the eye's blades. Some small wind shoves
the grass as if a snake were sidling.
                         The parents are heads down.
Their muscles move with each other as if they were making love.
Round he goes, and round she goes, a buzzard's marriage
on a thermal. Then a cry goes up as if the soil were screaming
or the wind were wounded on nails of brittle straw. A cry
neither parent has heard and cannot stem with any known thing,
not milk or love or kiss or words or food. The young doctor
from across the glen hears the child's call across five miles.
He rides towards it as if the cry were a fire rising in the fields
but all his knowledge's clear water will not quench the child.

And so it goes for the fever of three thickening months
except at the wick of midnight when the baby closes down
as if his switches had been thrown, or some wires scissored
in his throat. Tethered by their child, the parents thaw into sleep
only to freeze awake at dawn as the cry bursts back alight.
Folk keep away. Folk catch that cry in their cattle's eyes; taste

its scum in their milk and mutton.
                              At summer's flow, the postman
deaf with listening to a lifetime's stories, strode into their cottage,
downed a dram, and drank the scene into his memory: salt water
damming a child's throat, a cry that would not cease for love.
He stayed with him all day. The parents scrammed for provisions
and the cure of quiet. As the door slammed and their footfalls
slapped into the lane, the postman turned to the baby and the baby
sat up asking if they had gone and, if his parents had gone
would that now mean he could get up at last – and get up he did
as if he were a young man sternly sick of his own board and bed.
He could stand and speak. The child's voice was dark and thrown
as if four corners of the room were talking with him or through him.
The child clenched the whiskey bottle and downed enough to throw
a horse. He drew a long straw and slit it to the note of a flute.
Then he played the long day through, making the postman drink
deeper and harder than he had the head or height or heart for.

A moon widened on the windows; a garden gate squeaked
cringing on its hinges; the parents poured through the door
to find their child crying in his cot like a seal left on some low ledge
of the Atlantic; and the postman pointing at him, adrift or bereft.
'He's not here, your child. He's not anywhere. He's taken away.
He told me everything, how you left him to the cloud and sky,
left him to the harebell and the grasshopper and the cow parsley,
left him in grazed gaps between grass, to skylark and to hoverfly,
while you worked, if that's what you were doing.'
                                                They knew
one cure, one pure matter passed from their grandmothers.
When midnight massed itself over breakers and shore,
when the tide of the day had flown, mother, father and friend
headed by torchlight up the headstream on the high moor.

The mother slides her fairy-baby towards the waterfall's brink,
taut-shawled, his baby arms pinioned like a wrapped cat.
The child's mewling, breathing the breath of the chilled spray
slaping up from the trout-brown pool at the fall's foot.
The father and their friend are behind her, egging her on,
baying that it's for the best, that their child isn't in the child.
The moon bends a bow behind a cloud-castle then shoots
its light-arrow through a slit across the waterfall's rim.

Romany Sarah

Saintes-Maries-de-la-Mer AD 42

for Tim Liardet

Three girls squat in an open boat with air for oars.
A slew of sky foams into a sail as rinsed horizons rise
towards the sisters of the Virgin fleeing the Holy Land:

Mary Jacobe and Mary Salome. If this were painted
there'd be cirrus shaping itself into fingers of destiny;
heaven's afterglow anointing their solemn, upturned faces.

For truth we might paint in their girl, Romany Sarah –
watchful, wakeful, surf-splattered in the stern,
her sack of stiffened bread salt-spoiled, clung close.

Come closer. Sit by her. Observe her eye for surfacing
fish shoals – Sarah's lines and hooks chasing shivers
of silver sardines in their dolphin-driven bait balls.

*

The marsh is seething by noon. Mosquitoes stab darts
into wrists and faces. Landfall. It feels more a visitation
for the wretches in that coastal village. Sarah hands out fish.

One mother begs of her, 'There is more of our blood
churning in the flies' hearts than runs in our own babies.
Summer seres us. This is no port for your grace or your sisters.'

Servant and sisters sleep offshore in their slight boat
beyond the blood-scent of the mosquitoes. By morning
the coast is milling with a million swifts and swallows…

Air clears as though its sky of flies had been swept wide
like swart curtains. Taking nothing from their boat except
their clever girl, the sisters step confidently on to the quayside.

The Circling Game

John hammered and hammered hell-hot iron on his anvil.
Work was slow in the water that summer so what work he had

he struck more art into it. These horseshoes were a set, a double-set,
a dapper pattern, a gift for some girl he had long had his eye on.

There was a slap at the open smithy door and in loped
this lad, not more than sixteen by his skin and under his arm

a woman all wrought wrong like she'd been raddled under a wagon.
The lad asked, 'Let me a loan of the fire, bellows, anvil and hammers;

and let me work here alone.' Later the lad looked in on John.
The girl had been made right. She looked more than mended.

John fetched five guineas from him for that fire and free hour.
'But don't be doing as you spy others doing. The tatcho drom

to be a jinney-mengro is to shoon, dick and rig in zi,' the lad warned
holding the girl's arm as he left. John had a mind to try the lad's trick,

so tranced up he was by the art of it. He sized up his fresh horseshoes,
squinted through the nail-eyes, all over their harped, heavy angles.

Those shoes might have proved half the art he needed for love
but John had a hidden, beaten shame in him – a hair-wide snick

in his soul's steel. He couldn't court the girl with such work.
He doused the smithy-fire, hooped the eight hot rings on a wire

with his hope and walked across the valley to the town for a drink.

The tatcho drom to be a jinney-mengro is to shoon, dick and rig in zi: the true way to be a wise man is to hear, see and bear in mind

A fair was in town. There were posters tigering the shop-windows
and streetlamps. A horse-river ripped through lanes and ginnels.

Cobbles chuckled, shined under that iron tide. Street-silt, sheep-muck
and salt-grit from a slown winter shook up dust devils and mare's tails.

Rainbow tents and caravans flowered in the river-meadows.
John ran through them to hear their colours, to smell canvas slapping,

guy-ropes springing and pinging on pleached pegs, wounding
scents of grasses into his nostrils, making the penned ponies slaver.

John strove to stand square, to glimpse between dazzling horsecloths,
for there were horses here that John might as well imagine as see

– Andalusians, Spanish Barbs, Lipizzans, Camargues -
three thousand or more with their masters and flexing foals.

And children. The streams, the becks, the waterfalling children
bucketing like water from slamming caravan doors. The horsefair

ran with children. One sleet shout could freeze them before
they thawed to laughter. John looked out over the fair's field.

He thought he was witnessing the world or one bright field of it
with old counties buried but still breathing beneath counties.

When work was slow in the water you could go and come and go
through the mirrors of these fairs. John's hammer and hardware

hung jangling on his work-belt. There was always luck to a fair.

The fair roved every other week. It was as if the tall tents tucked
up their skirts and scuttled from one field to another. So quick

and sprack and spry were these moonlit flits from village to village
the tent-pegs had barely pushed down a first root before being plucked.

The Gypsies' wagons evicted curlews from their sites. For two weeks
they havered within hearing of each other. The sorrow-flutes

of the birds bubbled and purled over fenland and moorland.
Three skiving summer months John wrestled with, then won,

the trust of the hooves of high horses. For the shyer creatures
he played them the circling game – the send, the allow and the bring back –

then they'd nuzzle him softly for sugar and his salve for whip-cuts.
That gave John the nod of the horse masters, and means for meals,

yet money flapped about the fair, not a note of it settling near John.
He could sniff the stuff wodged in the pockets of the masters' jackets:

brash, burnished bundles of cash for buying up ponies on the spot.
The masters stank of rancid bank-notes. Their palms were plummy.

Their palms were planed purple with done deals and sure things.
John played a circling game with the horse masters, sending

himself off when wanted most, shying on the end of a lunge line
of their flattery, letting himself be talked back to the fair with a drink

before coming back and laying out the tackle and terms of his trade.

The horse masters answered to no man but their king, a Gypsy himself
who joined John as he worked, enjoying the sound and sight of skill.

As the days drew on, and John's silence drew him, the king spoke
of his own pain: how last summer his shire horses shied at an adder,

casting their wagon with his one daughter inside it, how since then
she was broken in body, blunt and blind. John asked to take a look.

The daughter was wrought wrong and John thirsted to find favour.
Months back, John had watched that lad gain a girl from the dead

with fire and hammer. He'd spied the lot through an eye-high knot
in the wood grain of the smithy door that he'd knocked out so

John could keep a look-out on customers with fast fingers. John coaxed
the king's pain from him with a promise he might mend the daughter,

remake her whole. And if he did, the king said, John might be more
than a brother to the tribe and king. The daughter was given

mashed poppies: stewed slurring flowers in a steaming steel mug
that slid her to sleep. Father and masters kept vigil in their vardos.

All night John had his furnace flaring, its bellows rasping and blasting.
The daughter's body flamed and melted. Her hair fled, flew up. By dawn

she was all dust. John poured her ash across the anvil. He palmed it,
gathered it, chopped and hammered it. John spat and mixed and waited.

He remembered he could barely remember a word that lad had said.

Cockerels were volleying vowels from valley to valley. John sensed
snaps and snags of twigs as deer drew darkly back into the woods.

The furnace grew cool and quiet. The daughter's ashes were damp.
John was weeping. He was already dead. He listened to the world waking,

eavesdropped dawn's massacres hooked in an owl's eyes. Below
cold clay's skin, moles waged war on each other, twittering, brawling

as blind as worms in their looped, lapsed trenches. John parleyed
with the silence with prayers. The dust stirred on the anvil's altar.

Blackbirds and thrushes broke their voices in the blue darkness
between tree canopies. Dunnocks drew bows in their throats

and fired music through the walls all around the silent smithy.
John knew in his mind there were nouns to each sound, prayers

in their pattern, noise with no name in the ear's echoing chambers.
What speck of the lad's spell had John not spoken? The daughter

was dust. Her ashes on the anvil were asking and answering him.
Then John heard a knock nagging at some distant door.

In leaped the young lad as though through the bare wall
beside the winking anvil. He blinked at John's work as if he were

staring through the blacksmith, sighting his soul's hair-wide snick:
'Man, it's not her. It's you need the mending. Didn't I tell you

not to do what you spied me do? Down tools and watch my work.'

The lad plied the daughter's dust and blew over those grains
until they glowed, embering on the anvil as the lad let slip

sharp sure calls, kind words and calm words. Shamed, John slid
towards the door wandering, still weeping. The lad turned on John,

'Man, go home and give yourself to a girl who can melt and mend
the tears in you. Love's the craft of it. The fire from its flint can bend

and make anything find fresh form. But let love circle you, mind.
Love's no shying horse for the asking and the shoeing. Send

love from you, as you have, and it will not allow that nor come back.'
As he said this the daughter's dust sparked. It spoored up between

the lad's arms as he lent art and shape. The daughter woke, melted
into life, leaning into the lad's neck, breathing his known name.

No Gypsy noticed John as he left, his tools still sulking in his hands.
When John reached home he gloomed for three months, then rose,

woke the flames of his furnace and frenzied a glow with his bellows.
Work was work, but what work he had he struck a lighter heart into it.

He sized up the old horseshoes, squinnying through the nail-eyes,
all over their harped, heavy angles. They were a set, a double set

with a circling pattern, a gift for a girl he had long ago had his eye on.
John tipped and hammered and tapped those deft shoes on his anvil.

Sunlight leant through the open smithy door and in strode the girl.

Camargues

I will wake up in a world that hooves have led to
                                        Les Murray

            for Fiona Sampson

Some horses are caves; you catch
that by the way they flicker and shy
at shadow. You can walk inside horses
and sense their walls trembling around you.
Camargues are air-delvers, the pile-driver
we're gripping on our reins, chiselling
granite miles. We caught their backs like luck
then held on. Camargues are not cave,
but they passed through like wraiths
slamming silently through the walls.

Thug-faced, hog-necked, anvil-hoofed
Camargues – necking the paint's hay
on cave walls of Niaux and Lascaux;
cantering behind the wasted warriors
of Rome, Persia and Greece. We rode
them here – or they rode us, chests thumped
out like wagons heaving our wagons;
warmed to our genius grandfathers
because they whispered to them
in horse and only in horse.

We should as well cremate ourselves
alongside our Camargues, riding them
through heaven's walls, hoofed pyres
to our Saints Mary Jacobe and Mary Salome.
We might have fired our horses
on our deaths as we fired our houses;
burnt ourselves upon the deaths
of our horses since we were their houses.
All horses are spells, but Camargues
are myth. You catch that on horseback.

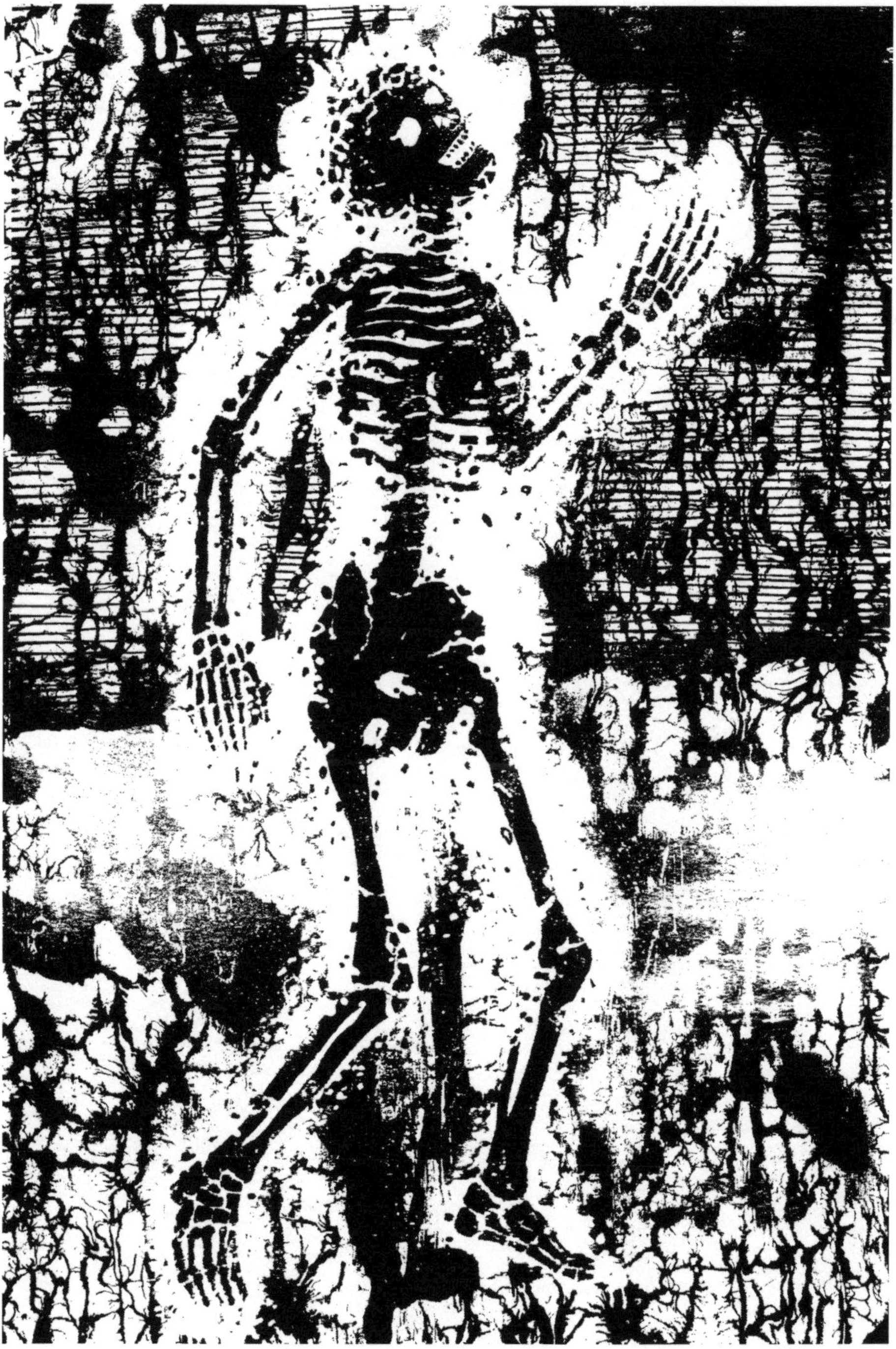

The Library Beneath the Harp

Papusza

Bronislawa Wajs, 1910–1987

At thirteen years old I was skinny, as nimble as a wood squirrel only I was black. I read books. My fellow Gypsies laughed at me for that. They spat at Papusza. They chirred about Papusza. *Your name means doll. You are a reading doll!*

I asked my family to enrol me in school. *Please, you a Gypsy girl and you want to be a teacher?* I asked schoolchildren to show me to shape letters. I always stole something and slipped it to them. Not far from us lived a Jewish shopkeeper. I stole a chicken for her. She showed me to shape words.

Years later, some Gypsies were playing music on a farm by a river and my stepfather took me with him. As I walked I sang, 'The water does not look behind. It flees, runs farther away, where eyes will not see her, the water wanders.'

While the Gypsies played their instruments, I read a book. Some gajo, Ficowski by name, sneered over to me and spoke: *Well, well. A Gypsy – and she can read! Now there's a surprise. I heard your lovely lament. I've been following your voice work.*

Papusza burst out laughing but I had tears in my eyes. He smiled. I showed him my songs. I sang my world. Ficowski said Papusza was something his people must hear. He said this so carefully Papusza almost loved herself. Her tears began falling in herself all for herself.

I approached the abyss. I told him about Papusza.
How it was raining. It was raining in her underworld.

gajo: non-Romany

Songs of Papusza

I was once besotted with a black-eyed boy. The young men
of my kumpania stretched him out in an àshariba. Only then

did Dionýzy Wajs, ancient Dionýzy Wajs, pay his coin and court.
He possessed harps, bought my mother and stepfather's heart.

All I possessed were secret books. Dionýzy arranged my bed
as we both wished. There will be no children, he had said.

This is what I swan-sung when I wed: *I am marrying
his harp.* I died back to life as a child, a bride at fifteen.

I heart-sang *The harp is the abyss. I shall never know
the earth again, not through her notes, not as the notes

from a thrush's three-fluted throat, or notes of rain
from a wrung spring sky, not notes of my horse's strain

as she clamps and cleaves the clogged road. I am nothing
but these fingers, fronds furling over a harp string:

those springing strings in my throat where the wind
of my breath wakes poems.* So the roads unwound,

my beloved books sly in an oilcloth beneath the harp
like prize tools you'd want wiped, spry and sharp;

and my voice swivelled, swelled, stammered on her song
while old man Dionýzy Wajs stretched and struck at his strings.

àshariba: a wrestling match; *kumpania*: a band of families travelling with horses and in caravan

Dionýzy Wajs folds his harpist's fingers, the fingerprints
wasp-stung while strumming his shimmers and feints

throughout the forest-villages of Volhynia. Our harps
are hauled upright over our wagons, like rigged ships

of music moving on breezes between those little ports.
Skilled mistrals finger the strings through starless nights.

We travel all day. We pay back the night with our numbers.
I sing at the dark while Dionýzy Wajs flickers and flexes.

My husband's harp hangs on a high hook. He tensions
the strings to one fugal tonne of force. He polishes

the teeth of its buzzing bray pins, the plane of strings
perfectly perpendicular to the soundboard. I sing

and his fingers follow me, melody murmuring on a thread.
He tilts the forepillar like a sight from which he can read

my every glance. A fleshy pluck, he says, will wake the warm
wan note; while a pluck from the finger's bone-tip releases

that strong, strewn soundburst: a drum's boom across the wires;
a door deepening on darkness; our windows as the winds slam.

At each stop we bartered my threnodies and melodies
for the orts of oats, lines for linen, for a mew of news.

In these villages, nothing happened but our music
until the Germans came. They murdered the menfolk.

We Gypsies couldn't flee for fear, nor fiddle for food.
We freed our nags from our carts. We wove into the wood

those heavy harps banging on our backs. We trickled into trees.
No water, no fire; hungers tensioning across frames and faces.

Chased by Ukrainian bandits, one Gypsy lad laid his harp's head
to the lie of the land. From that shallow sniper's nest, he shouted,

'We'll shoot all of you with this carbine!' And those bold bandits
outgunned by his humming harp, scampered downhill like rabbits.

Then a German came to see us: 'I have bad news for you.
They want to kill you tonight. Don't tell anybody but I too

am a dark Gypsy of your blood. God help you in the hell
of this black forest.' Having said this he embraced us all.

Everything was rags. We yearned to drink from the Milky Way.
Only the river learned of our lament, and maybe the sky.

For two then three days, no food. All slowed sleep-hungry.
Unable to die, we stared at the moon… I curse-sang silently

Ah, you, my little star. At dawn you are immense. Blind our enemy.
So the Jewish and Gypsy child can live, confuse him, err him astray.

Whose eyes saw us as enemies? Whose mouths cursed us?
Do not hear them, God, I cry-sang out to the night. *Hear us.*

On such a dark hark of frost a little daughter dies.
Over four days, mothers fold four small sons into the snows.

All the birds were praying for our children. Numb night came.
Old Gypsy women death-sang their fairy tale: *Golden winter will come.*

Snow, like little stars, will cover the earth, the hands. Black eyes will freeze,
the hearts will die. So much snow; it buried the women's warm bodies.

Years later, the moon shook in my window. She didn't let me sleep.
Someone looked inside. I dark-sang, *Who is come crying my kinship?*

Open the door, my dark Gypsy. Open the window where it bangs and glows,
where shapes with shovels are slamming and slotting the locks on savage doors.

You have come only for bed, for that would be bread enough.
You have come only for my song, for that would be dream enough.

Ice-lakes lapse. Linnets alight on flicked and flickering branches.
A lone lizard waits. Women from a village woke us from our trances

whispering that a war was won. We spied down to the valleys
where falcons flung their talons into the meadow's nurseries.

Family by family the kumpania fossicked from the forest's shadow.
We lit our first campfires. Nobody bombarded us from below.

Last year, I was panicked through a summer-sly woodland, chased
on three flanks by fascists. I kicked forwards at the softest pace

arrowing my feet between the pine cones' grenades, those hair-triggering
twigs. Hovering on haunches, I placed my held harp against living

bark before tip-touching the forest's floor with my fingerprints.
As if dipped in iron filings, manacled by a million tiny pincers,

wood-ants wove their ropes up my arms and neck, tilting me nestwards
with the harp's heaving wood a fat feast for these workers.

I ran and the red-hot ants hung from me as they tore at the territories
of skin and hair… Now we are told: it is spring again. The valleys

of Volhynia and Poland are veiled under dust from half-treads and tanks.
A red army climbs in a column. The linnets listen in their branches.

Havering hare, worn low by a hundred hidden harms,
I want to paw into the earth, lie fallow in my form.

The woodlands and plains were singing. The river and I sang
our notes as one word after another, the river stones enjambing,

poring over the poems of itself in whorls and whirlpools. Free to sing
we parleyed through broken Poland, the Red Guards punctuating

our road's unravelling story. For years my voice burst their barriers. I sang
in bribe as well as rhyme. I sang in time and I was always smiling

although my song was frozen as those buried children; although my song
whiplashed with woe and the whickering drones of the dead waking

as if blown back crawling from their bone-ash to my resurrecting song.
Unnoticed, we were noticed. Unwritten, we were written. That spring

I started placing my poems into printed pages, sheaves of silent song.
A gajo, Ficowski, plucked my poems from my throat as I was singing

and those children, grey-faced in green graves, broke into song.
How that cold country listened! How the grim guards started staring!

Sealing them into a book, Ficowksi's ink dripped over my songs
prising them into his pages' prisons – mute, unmoving.

Ficowski's key clattered in its lock. His footsteps fell away. I sang
to no one in the night of that book's covers, but I sang Papusza's Songs.

In this spell of a song there is a speck of poison. In that poison
lurks the white space of a lie. In the lie there is a proposition.

In the proposition – a blurt of blood; a dagger driven –
What is the Gypsy Question? asks nobody yet the question is asked again.

Papusza's poems point out that her people are problems for the gajo.
Like a victim seeking celebrity in his sainthood, Ficowski says so.

Those Gypsies should settle, they should be gouged from their vile vardos.
They have endured enough. Listen to Papusza. Ficowski says so.

Someone close to you betrays you so casually, believing himself
a favour-framer, a fame-thrower. I am called before the Council,

---

vardo: a Gypsy's cart or caravan.

the Gypsy Kris, for my sin against the tribe. Here, I say, are crimes:
I longed for love; I longed to live; and I longed to read and rhyme.

*I looked to the first too bitterly; to the second too slightly; and
to the third blindly. Love-thrawn, death-drawn, word-blind*

*I stand before you willing it your wish that I be cleansed
of all my songs and shames and poems and books and pens.*

The straw on which a Romany gives birth is burnt. A Gypsy dies;
the caravan with all goods and clothes is flashed into flames.

They're unclean. It's unclean to step over a hammer or scissors;
unclean to defile cookware with a cloth for cleansing the floor.

These things are burnt or thrown away. You cannot live unclean.
Dionýzy Wajs sits behind the Kris, unstrung, his white hair hanging down.

His caravan and carved harps are on fire; the scorched strings whine.
The chief Gypsy stares past me. His decision: mahrimé: unclean.

My tribe treads around me. The Gypsy children chirr like squirrels,
Your name is Papusza. Your name means doll. You are a reading doll!

   I am beyond my kind, beyond kindness.
                                  My heart is hewn in half.
   Now that you know me you do
                                  not know me. Listen to the harp:
   There is Papusza who sings for you
                                  and Papusza who sings for her kind.
   Now there is invisible, cursed Papusza
                                  stuttering on a stick through Poland.
   You cannot write of Papusza.
                                  She is without language or kumpania.
   These are stuffed in her mouth:
                                  a sickle, a hammer, a word-dagger.
   There is nothing to be said of her
                                  and less to be written or heard

or her own curse will course through you
even after Papusza curls up cold.

This is my answer to my enemies.
                                I am stained and unstrung:
your ink etched in every fingerprint;
                                my nails, their moons eclipsed
in your ink; each tendon torn, untethered
                                from its bone's bond. I grasp
this pen, and it ungrasps my fingers
                                as if I moved it with my mind.
Who is this nurse with her notes
                                her knives? I snatch at a hard hand
but it is already wriggled from its wrist.
                                Electricity earths through me;
I writhe on its bright rope's end.
                                Bronislawa Wajs, can you still hear me?
The doctor said this so carefully
                                Papusza almost loved herself.
The doctor smiles. My tears begin
                                falling in myself all for myself.

It is raining in the underworld. I stare back through a staring star.
I approach the abyss with my husband's harp. I shall tell him about Papusza.

Nightingales

The Gypsies wake in a woodland slown and slurred with snow
their eyes iced shut, fingers counting the cold's cost.
Somebody spades spindrift over the campfire's ghost.
Steam gasps from charred bones, from bone-white embers.

The Gypsies say they spent the night placing pantles for birds,
how they need to nab nightingales to trade at Christmas fairs.
There's a price on the crowns for those minds quick with melodies.
Winter nights in walled towns will ring with their airs.

This is what they say. The Gypsies can't explain the frozen doe.
That tarp must have been blown over her with those snows.
She perished of cold so they helped their knives to her.
They knew the danger, sure. Weren't they sleeping in the dangers?

All this is clishmaclaver to the bailiff and his boys.
The morning drags itself from the far face of a planet.
There are haloes arraying the stares of every star.
Their snow-tracks strike away together before they part.

A Lit Circle

All the world was inside this ring and the ring inside this yet

Inside, horses are slamming their heads and hooves against the canvas wall.
Outside, the canvas is red muscle rippling with their massed force.

Inside, the horses ram and rebound from the tent's strained skin
their nostrils flushed flared, their tails tapering under the heat.

Outside, the sky's firing rain as grape-shot, raking hedgerows,
knifing nests from branches, lopping leaves, exploding full flowers.

Inside, it's raining fire-balls from the big top. The king and queen poles
blacken, primed to blow up or flash-flame. Outside is waterfalling rain,

is edging across the floodplains, is mirror spilling out more and more
mirror all along the errors of dammed ditches, choked flood-drains.

Inside, the horses are seizure and slaver. Scenting the rain maddens them.
They try to hide, to vanish among each other, into each other. Outside,

the first fists of flame fling gold into the rain, into what will quench and quell.
Inside is escapeless, airless. *Outside*, the horses start screaming. *Outside*.

Rom the Ringmaster

Do you nav cavacoi a weilgorus? I call this a fair. *Ratfelo rinkeno weilgorus cav acoi: you might chiv lis sore drey teero putsi.* One poor farmer's pocket of soil but we've long pockets. You know farmers. Once, Gypsies were of use. Harvest-time. Hedge-laying. Now they've JCBs, migrant crews, gangmasters. Those fields we fetched our caravans to, they're blocked off now.

Farmers take six or seven big old bins crammed with concrete, hardcore, then JCB the bins into a block our vans can't jab round, not without a scratch so we don't bother. When they wanted us, farmers left the country on a latch: lane-gates and field-gates, front doors, even their larders and ladies.

What's gone's goodwill along with the work. Gypsies blame the migrants. White work-shy folks blame both. Round it goes, this hate, hurtling around. The question is where's that hate going to hurtle when it's without home, when there's no tober to tie the big top to, or job to keep the baby in the
bathwater?

But this field's ours for a fortnight. This is where wide England will walk, squat itself down then watch us and wonder. Here, around this circle of grass.

The stage-names of some of the circus people are taken from Bulgarian Gypsy dialects. *Rom*: true Gypsy; *Zhivàkos*: quicksilver; *Harlò*: sword; *Kasheskoro*: woodworker; *Stiptsàr*: miser; *Mashkàr*: the centre; *Saydimè*: respected; *Moolò*: dead man

Do you nav cavacoi a weilgorus? Ratfelo rinkeno weilgorus cav acoi: you might chiv lis sore drey teero putsi: Do you call this a fair? A very pretty fair is this: you might put it all into your pocket, a Romany saying from the *Book of the Wisdom of the Egyptians*; *tober*: a circus ground – 'tober' is Parlari, the British circus language which is partly derived from Romany and is not a written language

Zhivàkos the Horseman

This circle of grass needs to be sited just right – superlevel, softhard, southnorth.
Horses are picky. Shires, Shetlands, they've attitude just like you and me.
Making circus isn't about our own people's pleasures, not when there are beasts.
Beasts come first and last. On a one to ten the horses are eleven, twelve.
We've a camel too, scatty skutsome creature, who thinks she's horse.

The circle needs to be compass-correct, that means me standing centre
while the ringmaster strides around me with string and a hundred stakes
one hammered in every two paces, every two paces one hammered in.

Then we rig everything around the ringside in old order, the big tent,
four king poles, twelve queen poles, all the spaghetti of the electrics,
spotlights, winches, pulleys, the silver thread, stalls, circle, costumes, mirrors…

Then we might think about eating unless the animals need foddering first
which falls to me and my boy who's over there with his whip. That's him
snicking grass from the ground, from its sockets. That's his first trick.
In a year my boy'll have twenty tricks. Then he'll be after my act.

skutsome: sharp

Demelza Do-It-All

After my act as barrel-walker there's my turn on the silver thread, more subtle
than my turn with those fantailed doves, dementing dogs or hoop-hurling.
I do ten acts solo, six more with my sister starring as *The Starlight Sisters*.

I look in that mirror with that big hundred-watter and I don't know myself.

That's eleven different names, that's sixteen costume changes and they say
we don't work hard. That's what the police said when they gave the Court Order.
'Left the matter in our hands.' One day's notice to strike camp and shove off.

The act with the glitterball, that's my favourite, when I'm up in that steel star
swirling sixty spins a minute for a full two minutes, and that glitterball's
spattering silver stars over my body until I'm almost imaginary. Dazzling.

What's hardest is a hurt, sprains say, crying cramped in the caravan for weeks
overhearing applause from the canvas through the open door, that's pain,
or hearing the claps of rain on the van's roof when the show's over.

I was down in the industrial estate with my sister for small animal food,
the vet for the dogs. There are swastikas scratched on every circus poster.

Colin Clown

On every circus poster, let's face it, my face. Not Mick's face. Not Mike's face. Why is that? Is it because I am so handsome? You can say that again. Is it because I am so handsome? There's international clown code in that decision. Each clown has his face painted on to an eggshell and no two eggs are alike. Which is why I'm up in lights on the town's lampposts and not Mick or Mike.

I've heard some horror stories about this town. Have you heard the one about the bent coppers? In the end they used pliers. I've been promoted. Mick and Mike got nabbed with their mitts in the mopus, so. I am Pierrot.

Arlecchino, Pierrot and Auguste. Mike and Mick swiped the first parts but I was an august Auguste. I was the straight man the audience likes who catches the first pie or bucket but doesn't pine or make a racket.

I am Arlecchino. Where is Auguste now? I am afraid of Mick and Mike but their faces lied. They work somewhere dead now, like Shropshire.

What's that noise? Is the cat at the door or the wind? Or the wind's cats? My face is clean. My hands are clean. I'm dead. It's raining dogs out there.

Harlò the Watchman

Dogs out there are clamouring. Half the night they've lurched on their leashes.
I'd call the police if it weren't for the coppers lurking out there, off-duty.
I've spied their ski-masks. Seen the bushes bob and shift as they size us up.
Watched a squad car swallow its blind eye, probably bringing in supplies,
baseball bats, bike chains, burgers and the like. They are counting us up
while drumming up their numbers. That's the grapevine, the buzherimos
down the pubs. Not every gajo loathes a Gypsy. Not when they're circus.

Long nights are long nets catching bats, bats catching moths and me
watching, catching everything, drinking, watching. Watching headlights
squirming around the roundabout before stopping, dimming, winking.
I don't like the bushes shifting. I don't want to go where my thoughts
move with bushes. Half of me wants the rumble, the other half is running.

I've no tricks, you see, no act. White lie. I had an act, half an act counting
my brother. But you can't catch me now, brother, as I rise into the air
from my trapeze. You were flying to me, grinning, when both of us caught air.

Up 'is a signal in the circus, when acrobats are working together. "Up!" they say to give the command that they are ready for the next movement', writes Nell Gifford in *Josser*; *buzherimos*: gossip

Kasheskoro the Carpenter

Caught air. Caught light. Caught art. Caught sound. Caught song.
A circus catches the lot in one lit circle. And who makes it, mends it,
lights and strikes it? Nobody rigs a rope and tackle like Kasheskoro!

They approach me with the parley of a day's pay. *Can this be done?*
It cannot be done, not without miracle, balance and my just-right joint.
Structure stretches on a thread. It streams across air that billows

with damage. So: I plane and saw, saw and plane. Chamfer. Dovetail.
I say to them the wide world whirls on a thread. Health's on a thread.
Wage is on a thread. Friendship, loyalty, love. They all need craft.

What I need is MDF, meticulous method, and then you're laughing.
Then you'll have your illusion that Demelza's dangling by her teeth;
that the clown's taking flight even though he's as fat as the big top.

My trick is to make centimetre-certain none of you are caught out
or take the big drop, or flip the wrong flop. Nobody must know
that their dream depends on the dovetails and details of Kasheskoro.

Stiptsàr the Stilt-man

Kasheskoro upped
and offed at dawn
taking his toolkit
and trade, not waiting
on his wage. A plain
van came down on
the camp skidding shyly
on the frost, window
down. White words
were spoken. Birds
cued up their chorus.
One cigarette, and
the carpenter was gone,
sawdust still stuck
to his stockinged feet.
We're down three men.
Mike and Mick were
given the shove.
Somebody is counting
us down. I see all this
in my stride, hear all
this from below, where
my false shoes show
under those pinstripes
like drainpipes. Trust
me. There is a talent
to being tall. Why is
the stilt-man trusted?
I am the accountant.
Every pang of change
in the till, every page
of banknote, I feel and
read. Even the Ring-
master asks about pension
contributions and percent-
ages. I'm careful. If I
stumble once, that's
thirty-five feet of falling
man at ninety degrees
to the second. I back-
calculate my steps to
the inch. I toe this
dotted line. I worship
these numbers and
have given my word.
There's no door I can
enter without humbling
myself before God.

Mashkàr the Magician

Before God as my witness, on the tip every one of my fingers
perch firebirds. You cannot see them, but listen. Close your eyes.
Hear their burning plumage. Smell the fumes of flaring wings.
Excellent. Now, open your eyes wider than a child on her birthday.

Do you not see crimson gifts? What are you waiting for? Flight?

We rehearse hard until we can play it blindfold in a dreamworld.
Watch as I wake this white kitten from my wrist, this burst of birds
from my breast, this absolute arrow in my heart. Mysteries.
Miracles. Marvels. Mashkàr, where did I lose my wand this time?

I play my audience lightly. I carry them home in my magic cases.
I make as if I don't care. I am weeping yet you will not smell tears.
Here's my cape and cane. Here are two traps, and a trapdoor.
Here's my map and plan. What is your name, Sir? I can find you
your future. You will die, Sir. No, Sir. Not me, Sir. Now, Madame?

I am talking to the space where their eyes will tear into time.

Saydimè the Strongman

Tear into time? Me-karèste!
                       I can tear into these phone-books, run a rhino on a lunge-line, cart this caravan till Christmas.
                                   I pelt through my stunts solo, eke some strength out for the first night and go out running.
                                              Zhivàkos's leading his horses in, all the Shetlands, Shires and big Arabs. Night rain's stuttering on the big top as I go.
                       That's when the masked guys strike, when me and Kash are out of frame.
                           That's who they were waiting for, to bust from the bushes, lob five, six firebombs through the flaps, then wrap the tent with its own ropes like wrapping meat in an earth-oven.

They're popping pictures with their phones, not that they have fingers for figs when I light on them.
                       Not that they don't crap themselves when Kash veers up in that van.
                           The canvas is caved-in candle-mess, locking the beasts in, gluing the flaps shut and whoever else's trapped there.

I aim my arms at the entrance. Like forklifting two tons of terror it tears.

Horses pour past me into rain almost carrying me on their shoulders.

Me-karèste!: Big deal! (Literally, 'That's on top of my penis')

Moolò the Musician

Where's Moolò? Here's Moolò. Why are you calling when I am here
where I always go, stage-left of ringside with my tin cymbal, snare drum,

tin whistle, my sweet loops of music, my white lies of sound that make
the big top vibrate or slow to silence when the silver thread's being strode?

Under my thumb the beat of the red drum and the applause ripening.

Woodpigeons unhinge from the hedgerows. Where the beasts were bedded
there are scraps spilled from the floors of heaven. Magpies spy and spring.

Curlews collect long keys to their low homes between the burnt grass.
Lapwings manage their manic marriages, low-diving, upside-downing.

One trodden ring. Yellow grass. Green grass. Black grass. Where's Moolò?

> *I am here where I always go, stage left*
> *of ringside with my tin cymbal,*
> *snare drum, tin whistle.*
> *Under my thumb*
> *the beat of the*
> *red drum*

and the applause of wide England where beasts come first and last.

Here you are standing centre.   Here, in this circle of grass.
Caught song, caught sound, caught art, caught light, caught air.

Spinning

> *But these two things shall come to thee*
> *in a moment in one day, the loss of children,*
> *and widowhood: they shall come upon thee*
> *in their perfection for the multitude of thy sorceries*
> *and for the great abundance of thine enchantments.*
>   Isaiah 47

1

I love those stories when the world they wake
whitens on the horizon of your own eye
as though another sun has neared us in the night
or some new star flowered from the dark matter.
They shift on a single movement of mind or image –
a suicide leaps into space but lands on a high ledge
where he is found by fishermen with ropes and jokes.
The man says he thought the night was his own death
and it was, nearly. His hair has sprung into white fright
as if his head had been dipped into the dyes of the dawn.

What's expected of me, more so because unexpected,
is that I will go on telling and making and spinning,
more so because I was guilty of the crime called happiness.
Stories for children when we know all of us are children.
And now that I possess only my own poised possession
that I shall deliver these tales from some darker attention.
There they squat around the fires, with their teeth glittering.
They are moving on from their roll-ups to their shared pipes,
from red wine to glugs of gold whiskey. They are settling in
as if they were waiting for some long haul between settlements.

They say language shows you, so my stories should show you
what worlds I've wound through, whose voices I've breathed in –
that smoke spooling from their mouths; the fire's smoke
swirling above them makes an understood utterance, a ghost
of what we see, what we pass through and what might be watching
us watching ourselves waiting. If that's too curdled for you
try truth. A five-year-old boy dies. His parents bide by his body
for three days. Then they fill a rucksack with his best-loved toys.
Another rucksack embraces the child's body. They drive to a cliff,
hitch on the rucksacks and throw themselves spinning off the earth.

What does their tale say about how much they loved each other
and how much their son loved and was loved? Their story
makes something cease in you. They drove as if going on holiday
in a campervan. They say language shows you, and this story
shows to me that truth and even love grow impossibly possible.
This is not what you have come for. It is not what you wanted.
Where is the magic-eyed metaphor that reverses them into life?
Why am I not spilling word-lotions into your ears that allow
these three loving people to meet in another place, laughing
and singing and unbroken? Why doesn't the story wake the boy?

My own story interests nobody, not now I'm on my own.
Making story costs them nothing but my drink and caravan.
It's the hour before I begin when the clouds close down
and I'm lacking of language and in a desert of image
and nothing knows nothing. I am not even nowhere.
Now the word-trail slows in my mind, my blood sheds
all sugar and I can recognise no thing, not even the walls
of my van, or who I am, or what I will later, maybe, become.
I used to reach out at these times, touch my wife and say
'my wife'; then I would come back. I would come back into life.

2

The fire may as well be language for translating the logs
from their green, spitting blocks into red pictures and paintings.
The children spy wide worlds from the ringside of the fireside
as if a circus were performing before them. It shows in their eyes
for it is all reflected there. I usually start the evening with a call
to calm, then a joke and a drink before I unleash the animals.
Animal tales first, padding around the fire just there in the dark,
now in the ring of light, and back again; I go out of sight
for the ending. Then stories about witches (the children dozing)
and so on to burkers and ghosts before night swallows my voice.

They say language shows you but subject shows you too.
Reverse that order of telling and you end up killing the evening,
sending the children unarmed into nightmare, startling
the rabbits of the audience with glare of monster and murder.
Yet one day, one day I shall never be there, not that I am now.
I stalk that ring of light. I know to toe around every twig.
I know when to lower my voice, and when to stop silent.
That's when I let natural magic have its effect – an owl call;
a dog fox wooing demonically in the wood; badgers scratching
and sputtering. These are not words; they are warier than words.

They are life not legend and sometimes they flout me.
They do not enter on cue. They make witty what is deadly
or horror from humour. Control. Do I really want control?
When their hearts are hearing me while their eyes are on the fire
it is as if I were the fire's brother, that we were a double act.
The fire came free (although children fed it until sleep).
Just pictures and paintings. We'd see them anyway in dreams.
What's expected of me is that I feed their dreams, lobbing
green blocks of words that spit and split and charm and char
while all the long, wordy night I am desperate to be doused.

What's fabulous might be a hedgehog spiny with rhyme
or a bride born from gnarled nouns. What's fabulous might be
darkness drowsing over a woman of words beside a waterfall
of words. What's fabulous might be an anvil hammered white-hot
with hurt, or Lipizzans held or hurtling on the harness of a verb.
Truth or tale, you've winnowed my mind many times too many
for me to be free with feigning, and now night's met my heart
and halved it. This is something I cannot say tonight, for tonight
is my last night. Tonight at midnight I am laying down my words.
I shall bury them beneath the embers of that brother, the fire.

I am sloughing the freight of fiction, the shackling story.
I owe this to my wife for believing in the one truth of me.
I am leaving the camp by dawn. I am taking nothing
apart from myself. The enchantment I offered as payment,
they will find it under fire. They will shovel it out ashen,
riven beyond repair. Stories are second chance. They repair.
They repay. I am broken. I want to try the truth.   So,
I am glad you are all here. I hope you enjoy your evening.
I was here all the time listening to you but now it's my turn.
Ladies and gentleman, and children. I am ready when you are ready.

Skeleton Bride

Romany

> *Light up, phabaràv, kindle the kind wood*
> *for the rose of the moon is opened; the camp*
> *nested in darkness; our dogs snore in their heap.*
> *Prala, you are chilled. Seal your eyes when you will.*
> *Those lamenting tents might then fall silent.*
> *Our women are waiting on your rule of sleep.*
> *Here, take my blanket stitched with flame.*
> *Weave what warmth you can from what I say.*
> *Keep listening, more like overhearing I know.*
> *Don't heed the wind's gossip in the trees. Those elms*
> *lie. Oaks over-elaborate. I have coppiced them all*
> *for my word fires. Here is an ember to light you.*
>
> *Here is a story to return you to the surface of earth.*

This happened to me and it didn't happen to me
or I spied it when I only heard it or found it
when it was given me through a greater grief.
Remember the creatures we crave as children,
living things we crush in our craftless hands? –
canaries in a cage we spatter with gravel,
conies we caress before trampling them? Well
there was this Gypsy girl, Vogi, all of fifteen.
Her father had snared her, body and soul,
clasped her as viciously as his own widowhood.
They travelled narrow lanes, shy of thoroughfares.
Forced into the open at horsefairs, he forged
foul lies about Vogi's wiles before striking camp.

---

phabaràv: to create light; *prala*: brother; *Vogi*: the soul

Their vardo fell under a fly-cloud of suitors,
none of her father's favour, each a horsefly
parched for the bloodmeal of a dowry. They rode
head down, hardened to the nail of the road.
Some of these lads stole, some moonlighted – bad jobs;
each had winter in their sights, with its clearer aim.
The father set sly tasks, testing them, or spun twisted
tales about his daughter. One by one, they dropped;
man for man he swatted them; but after each fair
a boolòti buzzed in the wake of their caravan's wheels.
Marriage had to happen; marriage had to make a shape –
'a sharper shape than horseflies'. The father put it about
that at the midwinter horsefair he would sell Vogi.

There was spindrift on that flint lake for the fair; an ice lid
a yard thick, and one thousand wagons moored on it.
Bonfires startled themselves into life, their hearts raging
boiling the ice below. As more vardos moved in
to make camp, depth-charges blew under skidding
wheels, hooves. Tench, trout, char woke lightless, peering
up through strange skylights hacked out by horseshoe,
hammers and the raging of those bonfire suns.
By the glowing midnight, that lake was a lava-mouth
on the mountain, its summit blacked-out. Violins fizzed
in the fists of masters; banknotes spat from palm to palm;
horses shuddered then slept as the whisper was given them.
Vogi watched, knowing the meaning of the following morning.

boolòti: cloud

Deadheaded, her father slept, a ringing vodka bottle
trophied on his chest. By late sunrise, Vogi
hared the high crossways striking for the city.
Splattered, manured, those high hidden roads unrolled
their trades, beasts, traffic. A ptarmigan warned, creaking
cackling, descending the snow on its stiff-sheeted wings,
a whiteness on whiteness. Those wheeling clouds, the hills
revolved around her as she paced westward. When the rain
rammed her, Vogi cupped her palms and mouth, became a well
flooding and clearing. When the headwinds harried her,
Vogi steadied herself. She held the hand of the hail.
Two bear shapes watched her from a bivouac's hollow.
Then they stood their whole height becoming bear and man.

In her freefall through frost, through drawn limbs of the ling;
through closed lids of harebells, through ribs of white roots,
through green shafts of sphagnum, black spoils of peat hags,
through undercrofts of moss, through the eyes of worm holes,
through the dead back of bedrock to earth's weeping chambers,
the bear-men gorged on her gifts: touch torn from her fingers –
the men ripped those golden rings; plucked her hearing
with two hands; scent and song taken with her tongue
with what she could not see. And what Vogi could not see
with her tongue were her song and scent in her hands
with a pluck of sounds beyond sense: their breathing hard
within her, with hard bear-laughter, their shoes rasping on road.
Glaciers grinding and bending around her forever, and then never.

No speech as the search party slung the calfskin on to the ice;
nothing for a wandering ear to seize on and shape for a voice.
No say. The sticks and rings of stones where tents were struck
spoke: shadow-fires of campfires circled Vogi's body. No wake
then but a watch: widows cast behind to see the site made clear.
Vogi's body stripped, shaken over with shale-oil and what her father
pitched through the hole of his vardo's door: two dresses
mazed with mildew, a bible, a baby's blue bonnet. Half-fires
were dragged, swept together to make a farewell on the ice where
before leaving, Vogi was tugged and dumped, the surface so bare
now after deep firing it slopped on its hasps. The widows knotted
guy-stones and flax ropes to Vogi's white wrists, folded her into the fire
then poled down until the ice-hearth tilted and whalebacked over.

Vogi rides that upturned boat of flame as it bows to the lake-bed
trailing whispers, cinders: sharp signals flaring to violet then out.
A fire's weight of light. Green gravities in that freezing water.
Vogi scuds the lake's floor, sends sand singing around the wreckage,
floats on her flax ropes swimming at nothing, the only currents
the currents of an eel's wake; rushes of debris in open mouths of larvae.
Slowly they awaken around her, drawn by her shadow where
all is shadow: *Watch a door opening in the dark above you*
as though you and I had been buried together without knowing how.
To wake. To reach out and find you beside me when I thought
I had lost you; that I was never to be allowed one more sight.
Not only a door but our windows wide with life; wake now and rise
for they have risen towards you, they have reached out and released you.

Vogi woke unbound, undrowning her breath against the weight
of water. She kicked and swum, tides passing through open bones,
gained the roof of ice, clawed until she gripped the brink
of that fire-hole and hauled up on one finger. Unbelieving,
laughing at the flax ropes eaten to bone, Vogi stared at the pebbles
of her feet, the rigging of ribs; held her bright skull and laughed:
laughed the rain's music, laughed stones skittered on an iron river,
laughed hagfish, larvae, laughed a squall of blackflies, mayflies,
laughed invisible waterfalls swelling underground after sharp showers.
And when this laughter was out, when this laughter flew up,
when it swelled within her and grew its own soul,
as if laughter held its own gravity and drew a world closer,
Vogi found herself standing and not hurting, and whole.

The snowline. As though a sea of summer air shored there,
shed its jade driftwood and withdrew. Scrub, gorse and fir
were bent into a springing dome, thatched with thick ferns.
Vogi worked the wood, marvelling at the latched precisions
of tree grain, knot and wood ring. The forest fed her. The forest
folded her into arms of roots while the roots' tongues whispered
to the lake below, taking in her story as slowly as a year's water.
The word of her fluted from woodcock to woodlark. Even a river
caught it, winding the word of her like a whisper between boulders
or a thrown voice within waterfalls. Pine martens snatched the word
of her like bouncing prey, bore it down the stairs of the mountain
to their young; and when the mountain was slown down, when winter
shred the forest, the word of her word wound into the ear of her people.

Vogi woke and rose from her home of stitched branches. Foresters.
Gypsies. Axes. They were a world away yet they were here before her.
They stared through her. Vogi smiled. She could hear everything;
even their thoughts were sullen streams from which she could drink,
cupping her mind into dream and fear. They feared her. Vogi smiled.
Her calm collapsed them. *Unravelled by your hands I am mended.*
I am broken beyond breaking. It has rained tears all year. The land
is sea on which the earth's floe is a raft far off course. All it takes
is one word of wind to snap this woodland from its mooring. The lake
is my daya, the forest my dado, I call on wind, my phen, for this word.
Vogi strode to the men, and through them. Axes crashed on air. She smiled
and they woke in their lit tents and houses. This happened to me.
I saw and heard her. She gave me this gift through her greater grief.

Even now, when rains ram her Vogi cups her palms
and mouth and becomes a well flooding and clearing;
when headwinds harry her, Vogi steadies herself;
she holds the hand of the wind; she strides into the earth's
floodplains and windplains; where the world tilts
at lake's edge or river's rim, she sets her body to that slant;
she watches how the weathers weave her, broken beyond breaking.
The rose of the moon opens; she clasps it, cuts it,
she folds it into her hair. Vogi found her way home
by making a home of her body that had neither the ropes
of muscle or the silk of blood, nor a whit of thread
or mort of mortar. She holds most as she holds least:
up from earth's centre she rose before me, unravelled by the road.

daya: mother; *dado*: father; *phen*: sister

Here, take my hand stitched with flame. I am burnt low.
Weave what you can from what I have given you.
Prala, you are warmed; the corpse-candle is dying down.
We left part of the world, brother, behind us on the road
when, tonight we traversed those woods, saw the hoods
and hooks of rooks and corbies twisting and bouncing
around the lynching ropes. Those carcases cawing in the trees,
they were our hanging brothers. We stripped them rightly.
We cannot strip their wrong. Seal your eyes now.
Seal your mind's eyes too. That sight had cut you down.
Let the fire flicker out, the flame tongues fall down.
Let my hand of sleep close the whole moon's flower.

Let your hand of sleep close the whole moon's flower.

Notes

'Hedgehurst'
My version drew inspiration from Duncan Williamson's version in *Fireside Tales of the Traveller Children* (Canongate, 1985) but is very much a free adaptation of the tale.

'Taken Away'
A free adaptation of a well-known Traveller and folk tale. 'The Taen-Awa' in Duncan Williamson's *The King and the Lamp: Scottish Traveller Tales* (Canongate, 2000) provided my way into writing the poem.

'Romany Sarah'
Romanies gather annually at Saintes-Maries-de-la-Mer on the Ile de Camargue to celebrate the myth of Sarah, the servant girl, who is their patron saint. *The Mythology of Horses* by Gerald and Loretta Hausman (Three Rivers Press, 2003) describes how in AD 42 two female voyagers landed on the shore of this town. They later became recognised as regional saints: Saint Mary Jacobe and Saint Mary Salome and 'legend tells us they drifted to southern France in their small open boat, a craft that had neither oars nor sails. Coming all the way from the Holy Land, they had with them only their servant girl, Sarah…'. A ceremony involves a procession of Camargue horses to the sea, and the submersion of statues of the saints.

'The Circling Game'
In an invented coming-of-age stanza. The narrative took inspiration from the rendition of this Travellers' tale in 'The Boy and the Blacksmith' from Duncan Williamson's *The King and the Lamp: Scottish Traveller Tales*.

'Camargues'
The epigraph is from Les Murray's 'Walking to the Cattle Place', in *New Collected Poems* (Duffy and Snelgrove, 2002; Carcanet Press, 2003).

'The Lucy Poem'.
Most environmental research depends on the establishment of a timeline: how far back in the history of the planet can we go to find information that we can analyse in order to make reasonable predictions? And, taking these historical timelines together, how do they interact and inter-twine? I first found myself writing about the future until I realised that such images neither consoled nor could describe accurately the climatic possibilities opening before us. The science of global warming alerts us to the realisation that such catastrophes lie behind us in history as well as before us; that everything

affects another thing; and that, however much we have transformed them, climate conditions are beyond good and evil – our weather is not a moral climate. In order to find a truer timeline for writing a poem about global warming, I began thinking about previous climatic transformations, and how our ancestral species dealt with them. I settled on the story of 'Lucy', the famous *Australopithecus afarensis* of Ethiopia dating to 3.2 million years BC, the heart of the Pleiocene era. Who were her family or tribe and what were their stories? Where was 'Lucy' going the day she died? In her mind – and it was likely to be a considerable mind – how might 'Lucy' narrate the world around her? Her world and that of other creatures of her time (including large predatory civets and mass populations of antelope) were under unimaginable threat. Unlike us, 'Lucy' knew nothing about it nor could she or her kind have done anything to prevent the coming changes. Our evolution came about because the world of 'Lucy' was utterly transformed – the activity of nearby supernovae caused the destruction of the ozone layer. The changes wrought to the planet tipped the Pleiocene era into the Pleistocene. What 'Lucy' left behind for us to unearth was her presence, not her name. Her presence was the story, a timeline that predicted our own present. The story and name of 'Lucy' represents our story but with these differences: we have a timeline, we possess a little knowledge, and we know that our ability to continue the story of our own species lies in our hands.

'The Library beneath the Harp'
The poet Bronisława Wajs (1908–1987) was known by her Romany name Papusza, which means 'doll'. She grew up on the road in Poland within her kumpania or band of families. She was literate and learned to read and write by trading food for lessons. Her reading and writing were frowned upon and whenever she was found reading she was beaten and the book destroyed. She was married at fifteen to a much older and revered harpist Dioni´zy Wajs. Unhappy in marriage, she took to singing as an outlet for her frustrations, with her husband often accompanying her on harp. She then began to compose her own poems and songs. When the Second World War broke out, and Roma were being murdered in Poland both by the German Nazis and the Ukrainian fascists, they gave up their carts and horses but not their harps. With heavy harps on their backs, they looked for hiding places in the woods. 35,000 Roma out of 50,000 were murdered during the war in Poland. The Wajs clan hid in the forest in Volyň, hungry, cold and terrified. A horrible experience inspired Papusza to write her longest poem 'Ratfale jasfa – so pal sasendyr pšegijam upre Volyň 43 a 44 berša' ('Bloody tears – what we endured from German soldiers in Volyň in '43 and '44'), parts of which are used in 'The Library Beneath the Harp'.

In 1949 Papusza was heard by the Polish poet Jerzy Ficowski, who recognised her talent. Ficowski published several of her poems in a magazine called

Problemy, along with an anti-nomadic interview with Polish poet Julian Tuwim. Ficowski became an adviser on 'The Gypsy Question', and used Papusza's poems to make his case against nomadism. This led to the forced settlement of the Roma all over Poland in 1950, known variously as 'Action C' or 'The Great Halt'. The Roma community began to regard Papusza as a traitor, threatening her and calling her names. Papusza maintained that Ficowski had exploited her work and taken it out of context. Her appeals were ignored and the Baro Shero (Big Head, an elder in the Roma community) declared her 'unclean'. She was banished from the Roma world, and even Ficowski broke contact with her. Afterwards, she spent eight months in a mental asylum and then the next thirty-four years of her life alone and isolated. Her tribe laid a curse on Papusza's poems and upon anybody using or performing her work. 'The Library beneath the Harp' partly borrows and reshapes some of Papusza's introductory autobiography from the *Songs of Papusza*, as well as three of her poems. The title of the poem was found among the opening chapter to *Bury Me Standing: The Gypsies and their Journey* by Isobel Fonseca (Knopf, 1995). I am very grateful to Dan Allum of the Romany Theatre Company for introducing me to the story of Papusza.

'Nightingale'
'Pantle': a snare for snipe (Lancs.).

'A Lit Circle'
The epigraph is from *Josser: The Secret Life of a Circus Girl* (Virago, 2000) by Nell Stroud, now Nell Gifford, owner of Gifford's Circus.

'Spinning'
The late Duncan Williamson described in *Fireside Tales of the Traveller Children* how when telling stories around a campfire, Gypsy narrators 'would move from animal tales to stories about witches... and so on to burkers [murderers] and ghosts' as the children fell asleep and night deepened.

'Skeleton Bride'
In an invented 'hex' stanza of thirteen stanzas of thirteen lines.

13